HAUNTED HISTORY OF THE UNITED STATES

THE HAUNTED HISTORY OF ALCATRAZ ISLAND

BY TAMMY GAGNE

Cover image: Alcatraz Island was added to the Golden Gate National Recreation Area in 1972. It officially opened to the public in 1973.

Core Library
An Imprint of Abdo Publishing
abdobooks.com

abdobooks.com

Published by Abdo Publishing, a division of ABDO, PO Box 398166, Minneapolis, Minnesota 55439. Copyright © 2024 by Abdo Consulting Group, Inc. International copyrights reserved in all countries. No part of this book may be reproduced in any form without written permission from the publisher. Core Library™ is a trademark and logo of Abdo Publishing.

Printed in the United States of America, North Mankato, Minnesota.
102023
012024

THIS BOOK CONTAINS RECYCLED MATERIALS

Cover Photo: Shutterstock Images
Interior Photos: Kirby Lee/AP Images, 4–5; Adolf Martinez Soler/Shutterstock Images, 6, 45; L. R. Photo/Shutterstock Images, 9; Red Line Editorial, 10, 35; Matthew Baker/Getty Images News/Getty Images, 14–15; Harold Ellwood/Bettmann/Getty Images, 16; Library of Congress, 19, 43; Lea Suzuki/San Francisco Chronicle/Hearst Newspapers/Getty Images, 20; PhotoQuest/Archive Photos/Getty Images, 22–23; Anne-Marie Hartman/Shutterstock Images, 24; Shutterstock Images, 26, 33; Jessica Bauman/Shutterstock Images, 28; Alexandra Schuler/picture-alliance/dpa/AP Images, 30–31; Gili Yaari/NurPhoto/Getty Images, 34; John Nguyen/PA Images/Alamy, 37; Stuart Cox/LatitudeStock/Alamy, 38; Jeff Tracy/Shutterstock Images, 40

Editor: Haley Williams
Series Designer: Ryan Gale

Library of Congress Control Number: 2023939623

Publisher's Cataloging-in-Publication Data
Names: Gagne, Tammy, author.
Title: The haunted history of Alcatraz Island / by Tammy Gagne
Description: Minneapolis, Minnesota: Abdo Publishing, 2024 | Series: Haunted history of the United States | Includes online resources and index.
Identifiers: ISBN 9781098292508 (lib. bdg.) | ISBN 9798384910442 (ebook)
Subjects: LCSH: Haunted places--United States--Juvenile literature. | History--Juvenile literature. | Ghosts--United States--Juvenile literature. | Haunted islands--Juvenile literature. | Haunted prisons--Juvenile literature.
Classification: DDC 133.109--dc23

CONTENTS

CHAPTER ONE
The Haunted Rock **4**

CHAPTER TWO
Alcatraz's Haunted Houses **14**

CHAPTER THREE
Music and Murder **22**

CHAPTER FOUR
Separating Fact from Fiction **30**

Fast Facts 42

Stop and Think 44

Glossary 46

Online Resources 47

Learn More 47

Index 48

About the Author 48

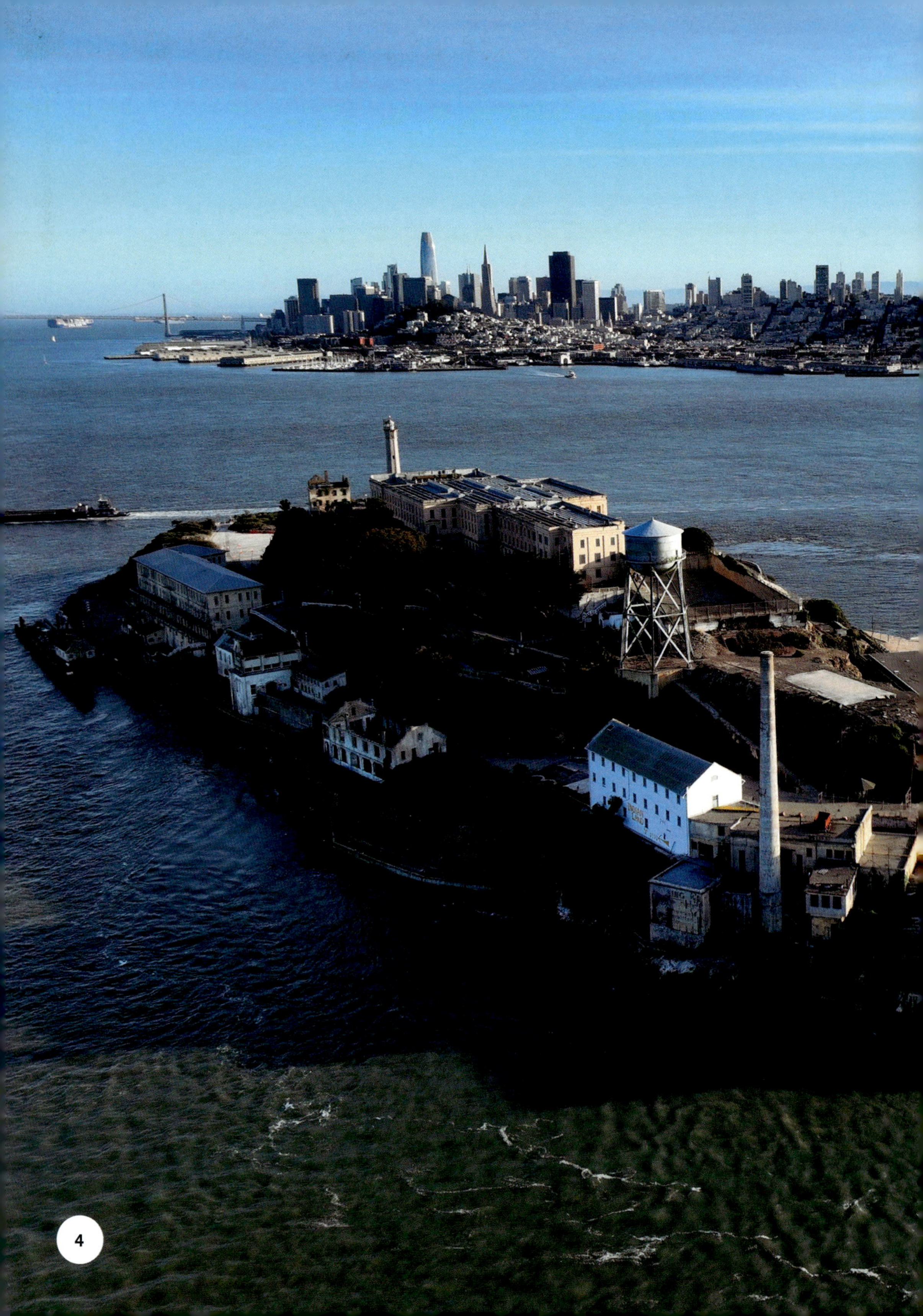

CHAPTER ONE

THE HAUNTED ROCK

An eerie feeling came over Sheila Sillery-Walsh as soon as she arrived for a tour at Alcatraz Island in 2014. The island is best known for its former prison, Alcatraz Federal Penitentiary. The prison has held some of the most dangerous criminals in history. Some people also think the prison holds ghosts. Although Alcatraz closed in 1963, it is still said to be one of the most haunted places in the world.

Despite her uncomfortable feeling, Sheila continued with the tour. An audio recording

Alcatraz is located offshore from San Francisco, California. The island sits within a body of water known as San Francisco Bay.

Most of the cells at Alcatraz were only 5 feet (1.5 m) wide and 9 feet (2.7 m) long.

played as she and her partner moved through the building. It told them and the other tourists about Alcatraz's history.

Like many of the other visitors, Sheila stopped to peer into cells as she listened to the audio tour. She snapped photos of certain spots with her cell phone. One of her pictures was of a visitation area. This is where prisoners were allowed to spend time with people who came to see them. Sheila could barely believe her eyes as she glanced down at the photo her phone had captured. When she had walked past the area, she hadn't seen anyone on the other side of the glass. But in her photo, she could see a ghostly young woman. The oddest part was the woman's hair and clothing. Both were in a style that was worn in the 1930s or 1940s.

A female voice had been playing on the audio tour when the photo was taken. The woman

PERSPECTIVES
THE SPOOKY CELLS OF ALCATRAZ

Lindsay W. Merkel visited Alcatraz in 2017. She later spoke about her chilling experience on the podcast *Confessionals*. Although she saw no ghosts in the prison, she described the cells as disturbing. She pointed out that their long disuse and decay have likely given them an even spookier appearance. "They are still scary places," she stressed. "Cramped, stark, and with no exposure to direct sunlight, the cells were bleak sad cubicles. The buildings were also long and shadowy, ideal places for things that like to come out in the dark."

spoke about visiting an inmate at Alcatraz. Sheila wondered if this was the woman in her photo. Before this strange event, Sheila thought it unlikely that ghosts existed. But now, she was sure she was looking at one on the tiny phone screen in front of her.

THE SPIRITS OF ALCATRAZ

Long before a prison existed on Alcatraz, local American Indians often traveled to the island. The Bay Miwok and Ohlone peoples believed it was filled with evil spirits. Many tribe members were sent to the island as punishment for breaking tribal laws, which are laws specific to a particular tribe. Some people were forced to stay on the island the rest of their lives.

In the mid-1800s, the US Army used Alcatraz Island as a military fort. By this time, it had been nicknamed the Rock because of its rocky terrain. In 1934, the US Department of Justice turned the fort

Many people believe the ghosts of former inmates continue to haunt Alcatraz to this day.

9

MAP OF ALCATRAZ

People have witnessed many things they can't explain on Alcatraz Island. Do you think the sightings may have been the ghosts of former inmates or the product of people's imaginations?

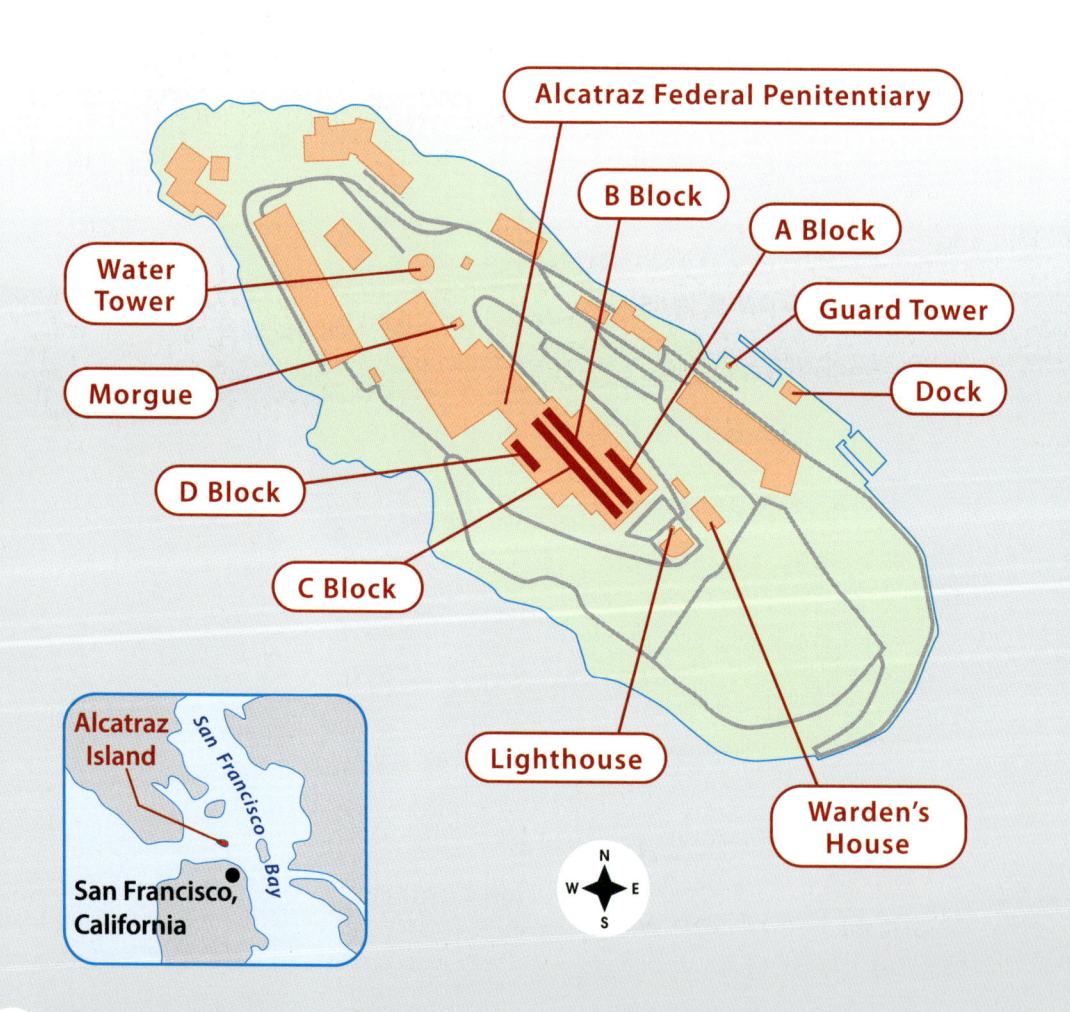

- Alcatraz Federal Penitentiary
- B Block
- A Block
- Water Tower
- Guard Tower
- Morgue
- Dock
- D Block
- C Block
- Lighthouse
- Warden's House

Alcatraz Island
San Francisco Bay
San Francisco, California

into Alcatraz Federal Penitentiary. All inmates sent to the prison were male. Many inmates who caused trouble at other prisons were sent to Alcatraz. It quickly became known as one of the harshest prisons in the nation. Alcatraz's remote location also made it a more practical place to keep the prisoners who would most likely try to escape. It was 1.5 miles (2.4 km) from the mainland. And it was surrounded by cold, choppy water.

Although many prisoners tried to escape, three may have succeeded. Brothers John and Clarence Anglin made it out of the prison with

ESCAPING ALCATRAZ

During the 29 years that Alcatraz Federal Penitentiary was open, 36 prisoners tried to escape. A total of 14 escape attempts were made. During those attempts, 23 of the prisoners were caught, another six were killed, and two were confirmed to have drowned. While there are no escape attempts confirmed as being successful, five men were never seen again. All five were presumed to have drowned, but none of their bodies were ever found.

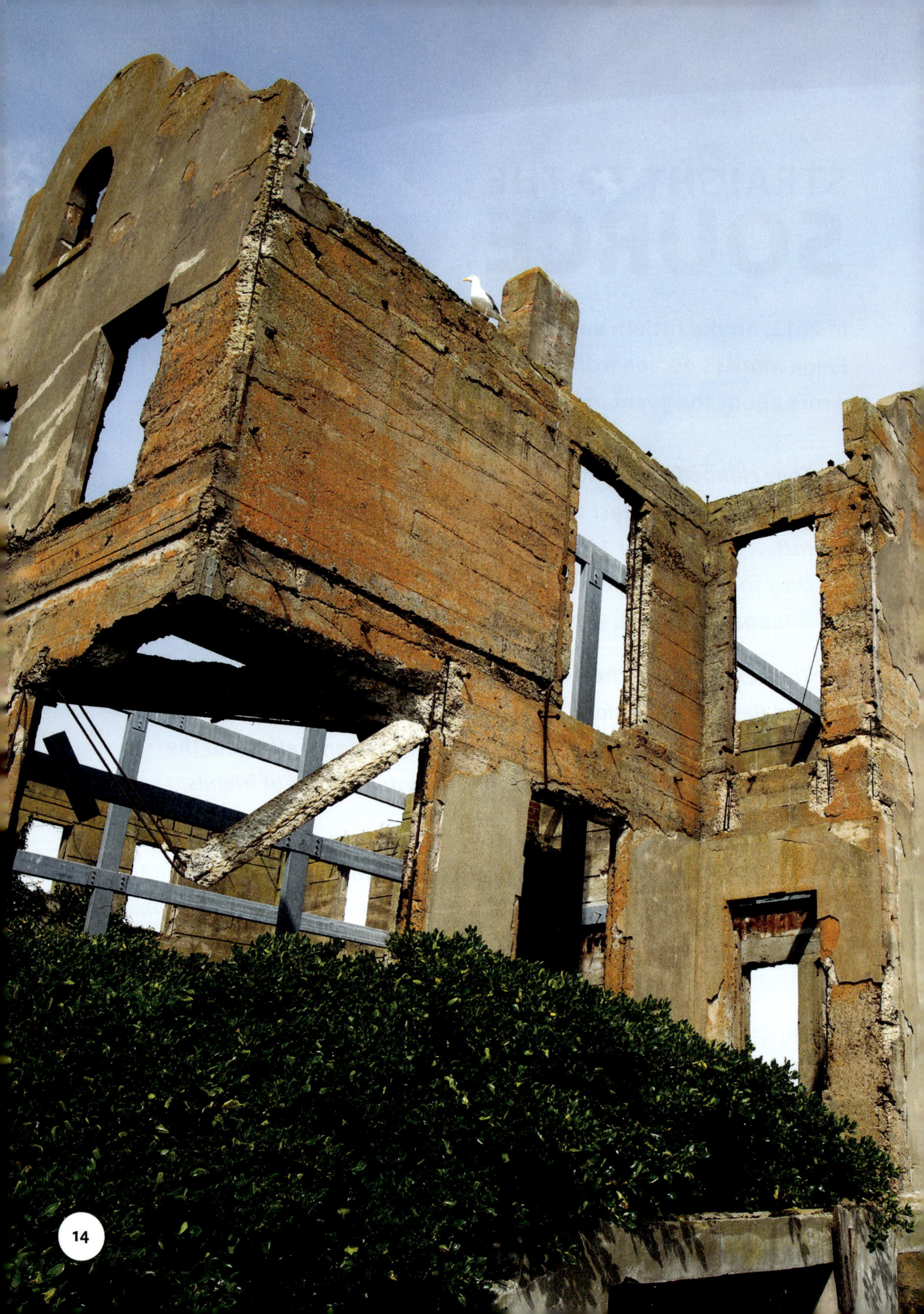

CHAPTER
TWO

ALCATRAZ'S HAUNTED HOUSES

James Johnston was the first warden of Alcatraz. When he started this job in 1934, he did not believe in ghosts. But during his time on the island, more than one paranormal experience made him rethink his beliefs.

Part of Johnston's job was giving federal inspectors tours of the facility. On one such tour, he noticed the sound of a woman crying. This was odd since Alcatraz had no female inmates or female corrections officers.

The building known as the Warden's House caught fire in 1970. Today, only the concrete frame is still standing.

James Johnston was one of four people to have been the warden of Alcatraz.

The inspectors heard the sobbing as well. It seemed to be coming from the walls. The noise followed the group as they moved through the prison. It got louder as time passed. A rush of cold air then came out of nowhere, sweeping past Johnston and the other men. The crying stopped as soon as the cold air was gone.

Another odd experience happened at Johnston's home on the island. Johnston threw an annual Christmas party at the mansion, which was called Hoe House or the Warden's House. During one of these festive events in the 1940s, the guests all stopped talking at once.

A man with an unusual appearance had caught their attention. His hat and gray suit were in the style of the Victorian era. He also had muttonchops. Men with this beard style grew their sideburns down the sides of their face but shaved their mustache and chin. Muttonchops had gone out of style before the 1900s. But the oddest thing about this party guest was that he was completely transparent.

Throughout the party, a large fireplace

FROM FUNNY TO FRIGHTENING

Johnston wasn't the only person who became a believer in ghosts while working at Alcatraz. When inmates spoke of ghosts in the prison, many guards dismissed the claims with laughter. But the guards also began seeing, hearing, and even feeling things they couldn't explain. Many guards reported seeing apparitions on the prison grounds. Like Johnston, some guards heard unexplained crying inside the prison. Others insisted they heard gunfire or cannon blasts. Some guards even said they felt fingers touch the backs of their necks when no one was near them. In time, many guards refused to go anywhere in the prison alone.

San Francisco is known for having a lot of fog during the summer.

Even after the old lighthouse was gone, some people kept seeing it on foggy nights. They said it disappeared as quickly as it became visible. In the

1940s, a guard was making his rounds outside the prison when he heard moaning. When he moved in the direction of the odd noise, an even stranger thing happened. The old lighthouse began appearing in the spot where the guard was walking. Out of instinct, he stumbled backward to get out of its way as he watched the structure come into full view. The guard was so scared by the experience that he quit his job the next day.

EXPLORE ONLINE

Chapter Two discusses the lighthouse on Alcatraz. The website below goes into more detail on this topic. How is the information from the website the same as the information in Chapter Two? What new information did you learn from the website?

THE INAUGURATION OF ALCATRAZ ISLAND'S FIRST LIGHTHOUSE

abdocorelibrary.com/haunted-alcatraz-island

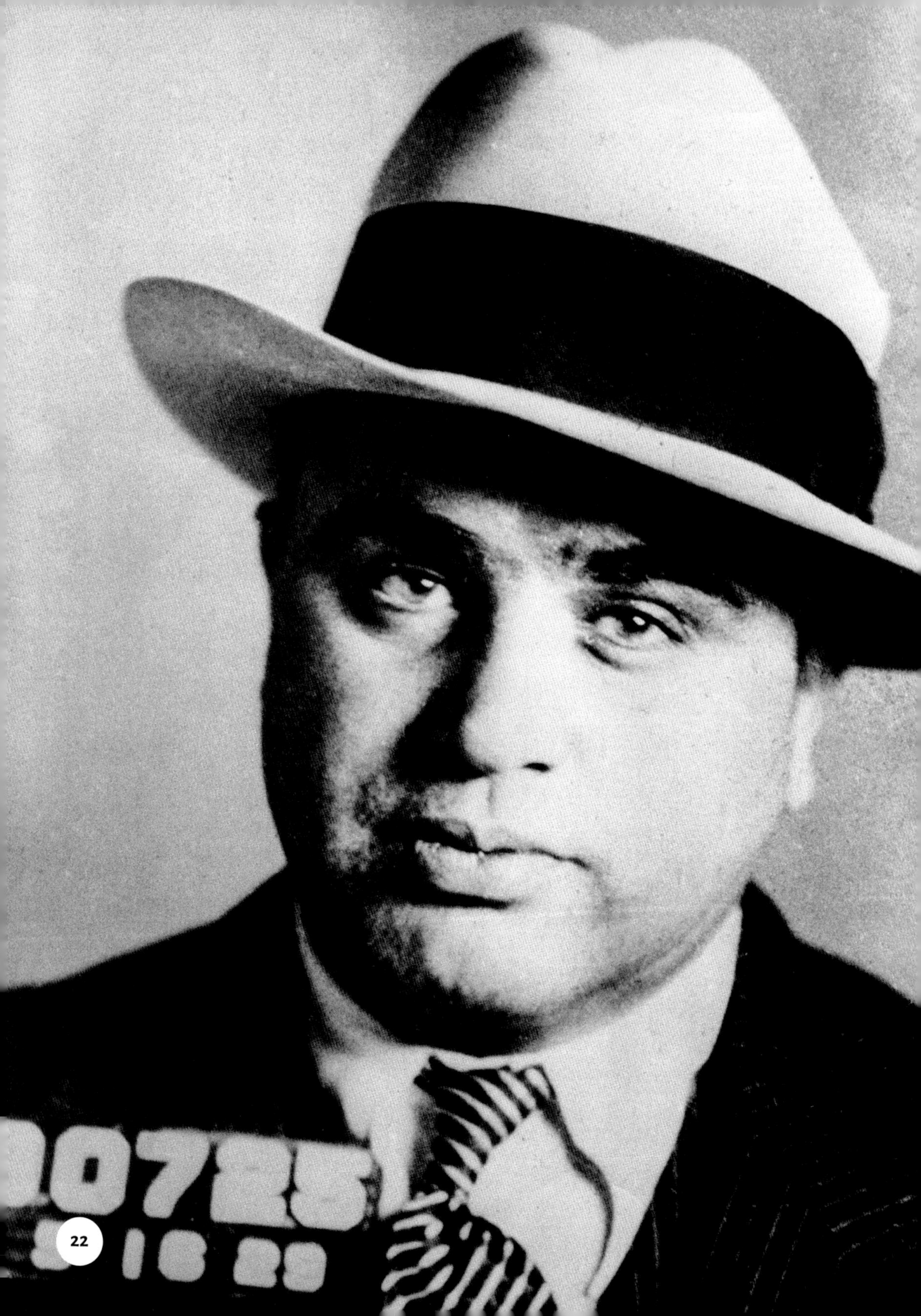

CHAPTER THREE

MUSIC AND MURDER

One of Alcatraz's most famous ghost stories involves crime boss Al Capone. Police investigators strongly suspected Capone committed many violent crimes in the 1920s. But without enough evidence of those possible crimes, the government charged him with not paying his taxes. He served five years of his 11-year sentence for tax evasion at Alcatraz.

Capone learned to play the banjo on the island. He often practiced in the prison's shower block because he liked the way the music sounded in the open space. The warden

Al Capone arrived at Alcatraz Federal Penitentiary not long after it opened in 1934.

Besides the cell blocks, the prison's shower block is also believed to be haunted.

allowed Capone and other inmates to start a prison band called the Rock Islanders. Another famous gangster named George "Machine Gun" Kelly played drums in the band.

Since the prison closed, many people have reported hearing a banjo playing near Capone's old cell, B133. A park ranger who led tours of the prison once heard strumming at closing time. He assumed a visitor had stayed behind. The music had stopped by the time the park ranger reached the end of the empty cell block. But as he left, the sound of banjo music returned. There have also been reports of music coming from the area of the shower block. Many of the people who have heard the banjo music believe it comes from the ghost of the famous gangster.

GHOSTLY GUARD OR PRISONER?

In 1946, six inmates, including Bernard Coy and Joe Cretzer, planned an escape from Alcatraz. The escape attempt is known as the Battle of Alcatraz. After attacking a guard named William Miller, the prisoners used his keys to free other inmates.

CELEBRITY GHOST SIGHTING

Country singer Trisha Yearwood had a spooky experience at Alcatraz in 2022. While taking a night tour of the prison, she and her friends took many photos. The guide even snapped one picture of the group on a small spiral staircase. As they were walking back down, Yearwood's friend Mandy snapped more photos. One was of just the staircase itself. When Yearwood looked at the image, she noticed something strange. A man in a striped shirt was standing beside the staircase. No one in the room had seen the man there before the photo was taken.

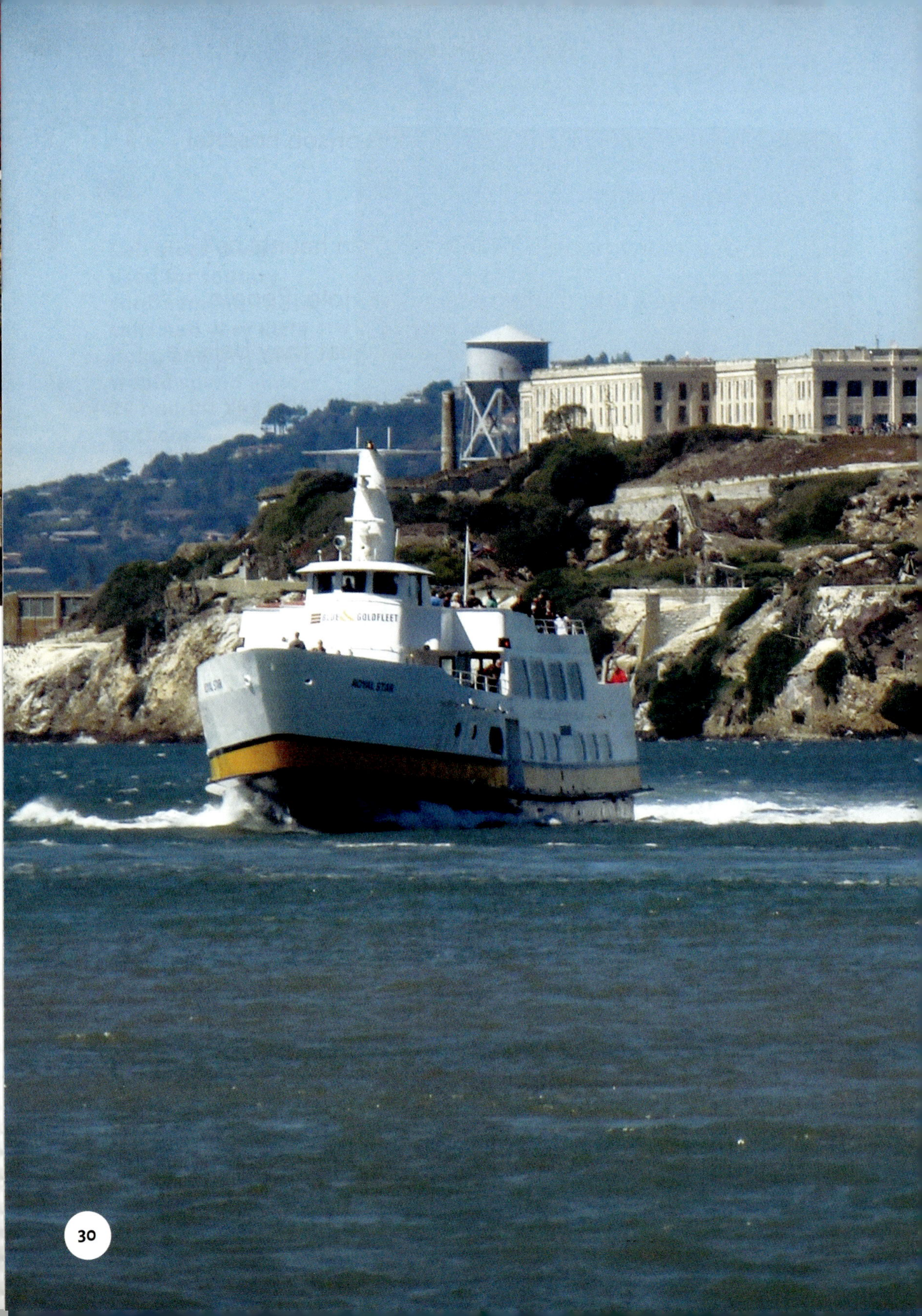
BLUE & GOLD FLEET
ROYAL STAR

CHAPTER FOUR

SEPARATING FACT FROM FICTION

Ghost stories often mix facts with fiction. The scarier a story is, the more fun it can be to tell it. But listeners may end up believing stories that have been proven to be false. This is often how urban legends come into existence.

One example is the story about the monster of Alcatraz. According to this tale, an inmate at the prison was sent to the Hole one night. After he was left alone, he began screaming. He begged for help, saying that a monster with glowing red eyes was in the cell

The only way to get to Alcatraz Island is by taking a ferry.

with him. But the guards ignored his pleas. In the story's tragic end, the prisoner was found strangled the next morning in cell 14D. This is one of the most terrifying ghost stories to come from Alcatraz. It has also been proven to be untrue. There is no record of an inmate dying in cell 14D or in this way.

Another popular story began circulating after psychic Sylvia Browne visited Alcatraz. She said she communicated with long-dead inmate Abie "the Butcher" Maldowitz during her visit. Browne said Maldowitz's ghost haunted the prison

PERSPECTIVES
NO DEATH ROW
Alcatraz housed some of the most violent criminals in history. Many prisoners died while serving their sentences on the island. Some were murdered by fellow inmates. Others died in failed rescue attempts. A few died by suicide. But not a single prisoner was executed at Alcatraz. It had no death row. Some prisoners committed crimes while at the prison that did result in a death sentence. These prisoners were transferred to California's San Quentin State Penitentiary for execution.

Abandoned buildings are often thought to be haunted because they look creepy and can make people feel uneasy.

because another prisoner murdered him in cell block C's laundry room. She described Maldowitz as a tall man with a bald head and beady eyes. The story has been retold many times, and these accounts often claim that prison records say Maldowitz's murder did in fact

PERSPECTIVES

DOING THEIR RESEARCH

In their book *Ghosts and Legends of Alcatraz*, Bob Davis and Brian Clune call the ghost story about Abie "the Butcher" Maldowitz one of the creepier tales about the island. But they find it odd that so many people haven't researched this claim that is so easy to disprove. They wrote, "One can only wonder about how a story with no basis in fact can become one of the most famous ghost tales from a prison whose records are open for anyone to see or why no fact-check was ever done."

for prisons. Many former prisons offer tours that feature this folklore. Tourists often enjoy the scary stories as they explore the cells. Many even hope to encounter a ghost or two in the process.

Offering haunted tours at a former prison creates a steady income from the property for whoever owns it. According to the National Park Service, Alcatraz brings in about $60 million every year. Some ghost hunters who visit Alcatraz record their experiences for TV or online shows about hauntings. These shows try to prove or disprove the existence

Ghost hunters often visit supposedly haunted locations to look for proof that ghosts exist.

of ghosts. But they also often inspire people to attend a tour while visiting San Francisco.

In addition to video cameras, ghost hunters use different devices many people have never seen

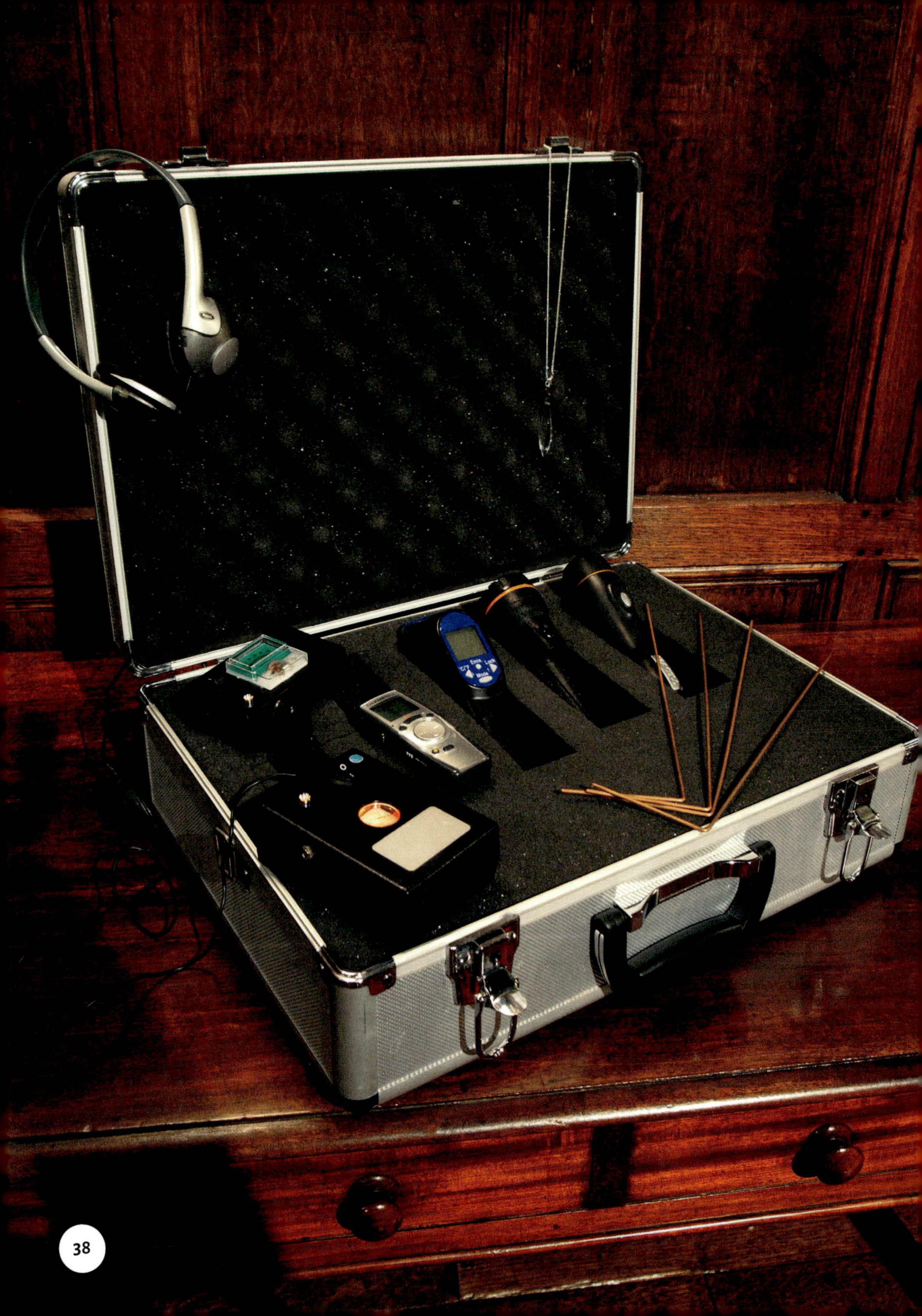

or used before. One is called a REM pod. This device uses an antenna and an electromagnetic field. The REM reacts with colored lights when anything with its own magnetic field gets close to it. Ghost hunters place the REM pod in places where ghosts have been reported before. Then they wait for the device to alert them to the presence of an unknown entity. When the YouTube show *Ghost Files* filmed an episode at Alcatraz in 2022, one REM pod suggested that a ghost was present in the visitation area.

Another common tool among ghost hunters is an electronic voice phenomena (EVP) recorder. It uses radio signals to create static sounds. Ghost hunters believe spirits can communicate with the living with the help of this device. The ghost hunters will often ask questions while playing the static. Sometimes they hear noises that sound like someone or something answering them among the static.

Electromagnetic field (EMF) detectors and thermometers are also commonly used during paranormal investigations.

Reports of ghosts on Alcatraz Island continue to make people wonder whether the old prison is haunted.

Debates will continue about whether Alcatraz Island is haunted. People will keep riding the ferry to the rocky island and touring the prison. Some may see things they can't explain. Others may insist the ghost stories are fiction. But these tales will likely always be part of what draws so many visitors to the Rock.

STRAIGHT TO THE
SOURCE

NPR correspondent Laura Sullivan spent a night in Alcatraz with former inmate Bill Baker. In an interview with NPR, she talked about her experience:

Alcatraz has a reputation for having a lot of ghosts. . . . The place is creepy. It's dark and damp and the smallest noises echo down the concrete hallways. The medical ward looks like something out of an insane asylum with old metal contraptions that resemble torture devices. All the while the wind is whipping through the broken windows and the fog horns are blowing in the distance.

Baker and I walked that entire prison, looked in every last room and laid awake in our cells for hours. I never saw any ghosts and he said he didn't see any either. I think it is the history of the place that haunts it.

Source: Emily Hellewell. "Beauty in a Place of Misery: Laura Sullivan on Her Night at Alcatraz." *National Public Radio*, 5 Nov. 2013, npr.org. Accessed 8 June 2023.

WHAT'S THE BIG IDEA?
Take a close look at this passage. What evidence does Hellewell offer about whether or not the former prison is haunted? Does the description of Alcatraz make it seem as if it could be haunted?

STOP AND THINK

Dig Deeper

After reading this book, what questions do you still have about Alcatraz? Find a few reliable sources that will help you answer these questions. Write a paragraph about what you learned in this process.

Another View

This book discusses many accounts of hauntings on Alcatraz Island. As you know, every source is different. Ask an adult to help you find another source about this topic. Write a short essay comparing and contrasting the new source's point of view with that of this book's author. What is the point of view of each author?

Surprise Me

This book discusses the history of Alcatraz Federal Penitentiary. After reading this book, what facts about this prison's history did you find most surprising? Write a few sentences about each one. Why did you find them surprising?

Why Do I Care?

You may not believe in ghosts. But many people do. Some even visit Alcatraz hoping to encounter one. This book describes spooky experiences some people have had during their visits. How might learning about hauntings at Alcatraz encourage people to learn the history of the island as well?

INDEX

Alcatraz lighthouse, 10, 18–21
Anglin, John and Clarence, 11, 13

Battle of Alcatraz, 25
Bay Miwok peoples, 8

Capone, Al, 23–24
Coy, Bernard, 25–26
Cretzer, Joe, 25–27

Hole, the, 28–29, 31

Johnston, James, 15–16, 17, 18

Kelly, George, 24

Maldowitz, Abie, 32–33, 36
McCain, Rufus, 28–29
Miller, William, 25–27
Morris, Frank, 12, 13
music, 23–25

Ohlone peoples, 8

REM pod, 39

San Francisco, California, 10, 35, 37

shower block, 23, 25

Warden's House, 10, 16

Yearwood, Trisha, 25

About the Author

Tammy Gagne is an author and editor who specializes in nonfiction. She has written hundreds of books for both children and adults. She lives in northern New England with her husband, son, and dogs.